STATEMENT OF
GENERAL CURTIS M. SCAPARROTTI
COMMANDER, UNITED NATIONS COMMAND;
COMMANDER, UNITED STATES-REPUBLIC OF KOREA COMBINED FORCES
COMMAND;
AND COMMANDER, UNITED STATES FORCES KOREA
BEFORE THE
SENATE ARMED SERVICES COMMITTEE

March 25, 2014

TABLE OF CONTENTS

1. INTRODUCTION………………………………………………………. 1

2. STRATEGIC ENVIRONMENT………………………………… 2

3. NORTH KOREA………………………………………………… 3
Coercive Strategy
Conventional Capabilities
Asymmetric Capabilities
Internal Situation
Outlook

4. REPUBLIC OF KOREA………………………………………. 6
Inter-Korean and Foreign Relations
Concerns About U.S. Commitment
Republic of Korea Military
- Military Strategy
- Manning and Budget
- Capabilities and Force Improvement

5. THREE COMMANDS………………………………………… 9
United Nations Command (UNC)
U.S.-ROK Combined Forces Command (CFC)
United States Forces Korea (USFK)

6. U.S.-ROK ALLIANCE………………………………………. 12
Strong Relationships
Alliance Transformation
Authorities and Consultation
Burden Sharing
Counter Missile Capabilities
Tailored Deterrence
Operationalizing Deterrence
Exercises
Readiness and Challenges
A Bright Future Together

7. VISION 2014 AND PRIORITIES………………………………. 16
Sustain and Strengthen the Alliance
Maintain the Armistice: Deter and Defeat Aggression –
    Be Ready to "Fight Tonight"
Alliance Transformation
Sustain Force and Family Readiness
Enhance the UNC, CFC, and USFK Team

8. CLOSING………………………………………………………. 18

1. INTRODUCTION.

Mr. Chairman and distinguished members of the Committee, I am honored to testify as the Commander of the United Nations Command (UNC), United States–Republic of Korea (ROK) Combined Forces Command (CFC), and United States Forces Korea (USFK). On behalf of the Service Members, Civilians, Contractors, and their Families who serve our great nation in Korea, I thank you for your support. Our enduring military presence in Korea prevents war and preserves stability in a region critical to U.S. security. The U.S.-ROK Alliance protects both of our nations' vital interests by protecting our citizens, advancing our values, and enabling prosperity.

In 2013, we marked the 60th anniversaries of the Armistice Agreement that suspended the Korean War and the signing of the U.S.-ROK Mutual Defense Treaty. The U.S.-ROK Alliance is among history's most successful partnerships, providing the foundation for regional stability and prosperity. For 60 years, our Alliance has succeeded in preserving the Armistice Agreement, promoting democracy, and providing stability for the people of South Korea and the region. The Alliance is strong, but we will not allow ourselves to be complacent – we are and will remain ready. In the year ahead, we will face challenges and opportunities particularly in adapting the Alliance to changes in the North Korean threat.

North Korea remains a threat that is continually increasing its asymmetric capabilities amid a declining, yet large conventional force. Kim Jong-un is firmly in control despite his family's legacy of failure and the suffering of the North Korean people. The Kim regime threatens the United States and South Korea, where more than 114,000 Americans reside. North Korea's actions hold at risk a regional trade network that supports 2.8 million U.S. jobs and $555 billion in U.S. exports.

Thanks to the support of our national leaders and the American people, USFK's presence is a strong commitment to South Korea and preserves stability and prosperity. USFK, a modern, capable, and forward-deployed force, stands ready to support our Nation's interests and defend our ally.

2. STRATEGIC ENVIRONMENT.

U.S. security and prosperity depend on stable relationships with regional partners and allies, and regional stability depends on enduring U.S. presence and leadership. The Asia-Pacific region produces a quarter of the world's gross domestic product and is home to a quarter of the world's population, as well as the world's largest military and economic powers. These nations face the challenge of interdependence, relying on the U.S. for stability while increasingly relying on China economically. In the face of strategic change and military threats, the U.S. is the constant that provides stability and a framework for conflict avoidance and resolution.

Security Developments. Northeast Asia contains four of the world's six largest militaries. Regionally, China has heightened regional influence while pursuing a comprehensive military modernization program. This development is taking place against a backdrop of historical antagonism and growing territorial claims.

Economic Center of Gravity. The Asia-Pacific region is an economic center of gravity indispensible to the U.S. economy and our ability to maintain global leadership. In 2013, the region was responsible for 40% of global economic growth, with U.S. trade increasing by 22% between 2008 and 2012. In 2012, exports reached $555 billion, a 31% increase since 2008 supporting 2.8 million American jobs. The region invested $422 billion in the U.S. by the end of 2012, up 31% since 2008. The Korea-U.S. Free Trade Agreement is providing tangible benefits and is expanding a critical U.S. trading relationship, one that topped $130 billion in goods and services in 2012. The region's economic prosperity, in turn, relies on the stability that enduring U.S. leadership and military presence provide.

The China Factor. China's reshaping of the region's strategic landscape impacts the security of both Koreas. While concerned about China's growing assertiveness and lack of transparency, South Korea is committed to deepening relations with China, its largest trading partner, in a manner that does not compromise the health of the U.S.-ROK Alliance. South Korea sees China as playing a critical role in shaping North Korean behavior. However, China's near-term focus on stability and concerns about the future of the U.S.-ROK Alliance render it unlikely to take measures that could destabilize North Korea. Despite strains in the Sino-North Korean relationship, the Kim regime continues to rely on China for resources, as well as diplomatic cover to constrain international efforts to pressure North Korea to denuclearize and alter its aggressive behavior.

3. NORTH KOREA.

North Korea remains a significant threat to United States' interests, the security of South Korea, and the international community due to its willingness to use force, its continued development and proliferation of nuclear weapon and long-range ballistic missile programs, and its abuse of its citizens' human rights, as well as the legitimate interests of its neighbors and the international community. Last year at this time, North Korea embarked on a series of provocations including a satellite launch, nuclear test, and the deployment of a road mobile intermediate range ballistic missile, all in violation of UN Security Council resolutions. Recently, the United Nations Commission of Inquiry on North Korean Human Rights detailed North Korean abuses, assessed their impact, and made recommendations. North Korea's growing asymmetric capabilities present the U.S.-ROK Alliance with a challenging and complex threat.

Coercive Strategy. The Kim Jong-un regime's overriding interest is ensuring its survival. To achieve this, North Korea employs a coercive strategy, using force or the threat of force in an attempt to influence the United States and South Korea. The Kim regime seeks to maintain internal security, develop a strong military deterrent, and pursue coercive diplomacy to compel acceptance of its nuclear program. Rather than seeking rapprochement with the international community, North Korea deliberately isolates itself.

The Kim regime's strategic campaign is calculated, but risky. Escalatory acts involving nuclear development, missile tests, and military posture changes near the Demilitarized Zone (DMZ) carry with them elements of uncertainty and the potential for miscalculation, and rapid and unintended escalation.

Conventional Capabilities. North Korea continues to place priority on its military readiness. The Korean People's Army (KPA) – an umbrella organization comprising all military services – is the fourth largest military in the world. It fields approximately one million troops; 4,100 tanks; 2,100 armored vehicles; and 8,500 pieces of field artillery in addition to over 700 combat aircraft, 420 patrol combatants at sea, and 70 submarines. Over the past three decades, the regime has incrementally positioned the majority of this force within 90 miles of the DMZ, where they are postured for offensive or defensive operations. This means that they can strike targets within the Seoul Metropolitan Area where over 23 million South Koreans and almost 50,000 American citizens live.

Asymmetric Capabilities. While North Korea's massive conventional forces have been declining due to aging and lack of resources, and likely realizing that it cannot counter the Alliance head on, North Korea is emphasizing the development of its asymmetric capabilities. North Korea's asymmetric arsenal includes several hundred ballistic missiles, a large chemical weapons stockpile, a biological weapons research program, the world's largest special operations forces, and an active cyber warfare capability.

- **Nuclear arms and ballistic missiles.** North Korea continues to develop nuclear weapons and ballistic missiles in violation of multiple United Nations Security Council Resolutions. Today, it fields SCUD and Nodong missiles that are able to strike the entire Korean Peninsula and U.S. bases in Japan that also support UNC forces should they be called upon to defend the ROK. It is investing heavily in longer-range missiles with the potential to target the U.S. homeland. North Korea shows little regard for the fact that the possession of, pursuit of, and threat to use nuclear weapons and their means of delivery are the primary barriers to its inclusion in the international community and productive economic integration.

- **Cyber capability.** North Korea employs computer hackers capable of conducting open-source intelligence collection, cyber-espionage, and disruptive cyber-attacks. Several attacks on South Korea's banking institutions over the past few years have been attributed to North Korea. Cyber warfare is an important asymmetric dimension of conflict that North Korea will probably continue to emphasize — in part because of its deniability and low relative costs.

Internal Situation. North Korea is a dictatorship under Kim Jong-un. He demonstrated his willingness to use his internal security agencies last year by arresting and very publicly purging Jang Song-taek, his uncle by marriage and a powerful member of the regime's inner circle. Though this event inspired wide speculation in the press, we do not believe it is a sign of instability – it was a calculated and deliberate action by Kim Jong-un to demonstrate his control of the regime.

Nevertheless, long-term trends continue to challenge the regime's internal stability. The level of military readiness places a tremendous economic burden on North Korea's population. North Korea's economy shows little improvement, and South Korea has declared that it will no longer provide substantial aid without first re-establishing trust. Additionally, in spite of the regime's efforts to control it, the influx of external information continues to grow. The regime will face increasing challenges to the control of information, which could gradually weaken the effectiveness of its internal propaganda.

Outlook. For the foreseeable future, North Korea will remain an isolated and unpredictable state willing to use violent behavior to advance its interests, attempt to gain recognition as a nuclear power, and secure the regime's continuation. The regime needs to portray the U.S. as an enemy to distract its population from economic hardship, government brutality, and systemic incompetence. Therefore, a shift to a truly conciliatory posture toward the U.S. is unlikely.

We remain concerned about the potential for a localized, violent act against South Korea, which could start a cycle of response and counter-response, leading to an unintended, uncontrolled escalation and a wider conflict. Also, we assess that North Korea has already taken initial steps towards fielding a road-mobile ICBM , although it remains untested. North Korea is committed to developing long-range missile technology that is capable of posing a direct threat to the U.S. Our Alliance with South Korea continues to be the critical linchpin required to deter North Korean aggression and to maintain stability.

4. REPUBLIC OF KOREA.

South Korea is a modern, prosperous democracy empowered by the creative drive and hard working spirit of its people. South Korea is poised to increase its regional and global influence to the benefit of both our nations. Against this backdrop in February 2013, President Park Geun-hye took office with a four-dimensional strategy focusing on Economic Democratization (domestic reforms to enable sustainable economic growth), the Trust-Building Process or *Trustpolitik* (North-South relations), the Northeast Asia Peace Initiative or Seoul Process (increase ROK regional influence and leadership), and Active Defense and Military Reform (counter North Korean provocations and threat). She committed significant time and energy in recalibrating South Korean policy toward North Korea, while she strengthened the ROK's international influence and leadership as a rising middle power across the diplomatic, informational, military, and economic spectrum. President Park is a staunch supporter of our Alliance, and she is committed to enhancing South Korea's ability to respond to provocation, and deter or defeat North Korean aggression.

Inter-Korean and Foreign Relations. President Park deftly managed relations with North Korea in the face of North Korean aggressiveness and leadership turbulence. The ROK deterred provocations (with visible U.S. support) and resisted acceding to North Korean demands. South Korea's management of North-South relations and *Trustpolitik* are moving ahead in a manner that seeks to avoid creating new vulnerabilities. In February, the Koreas conducted their first family reunions since 2010. This was a positive, humanitarian event for the families of both countries who remain separated since the Korean War. Through the Seoul Process, South Korea seeks to increase its international influence and leadership, and President Park held 37 meetings with other heads of state, including President Obama.

Concerns About U.S. Commitment. We are committed to the defense of South Korea, and continue to demonstrate that commitment with additive rotational units to Korea, extended deterrence, and priority in defense resources and emphasis – second only to Afghanistan. However, due to a history of foreign invasions and the continuing North Korean threat, South Korea is concerned about adjustments in U.S. security strategy, particularly about reduction of U.S. commitment or resources. Confidence in U.S. commitment will play an important role in how South Korea designs and executes its defense strategy, and postures and structures its military.

Republic of Korea Military. The South Korean military is a capable, modern force operating in an effective partnership with U.S. forces. The North Korean threat remains its primary focus, but Seoul is increasing its ability to contribute to international security. Beginning with the Vietnam War, Seoul has contributed to several U.S. and U.S.-led international coalitions, most recently with combat service and civilian reconstruction support in Iraq, Afghanistan, and South Sudan, as well as deployments to support multinational anti-piracy and non-proliferation operations. More than 1,100 South Korean military members are deployed to 12 U.S.-led or UN-mandated missions.

- **Military Strategy.** South Korean military strategy calls for a rapid and robust response to North Korean provocations. The South Korean military is focused on protecting its people, believing that a commitment to a firm and immediate response to North Korean violence is essential to deterrence and self-defense. I am concerned about the potential for miscalculation and escalation, and I believe that both our nations are best served through an Alliance response based on seamless and rapid consultation through mutually agreed-upon processes. To mitigate these concerns, we are enhancing our crisis management and escalation control measures through exercises and the bilateral Counter Provocation Plan we signed last year.

- **Manning and Budget.** The South Korean military has an active duty force of 639,000 personnel augmented by 2.9 million reservists. Demographics are driving its military to reduce manning to 517,000 active duty service members at some point in the 2020s. South Korea plans to offset this reduction in force with capability enhancements, including high technology weapons. South Korea has the 12th largest defense budget in the world with a 2014 budget of $32.7 billion. Although Seoul continues to expand defense spending – this year's defense budget represents a 4% increase over 2013, 14.5% of the overall national budget, and 2.49% of Gross Domestic Product – it still has not been able to meet the ambitious defense spending objectives of its current long-range defense plan, prompting a re-evaluation and re-prioritization of defense acquisition priorities and future force posture.

- **Capabilities and Force Improvement**. The Republic of Korea is making tough choices on military capabilities, attempting to achieve a number of security objectives. While the North Korean threat remains its priority, South Korea is also factoring the defense of sea lines of communication and maritime exclusive economic zones, balancing other regional powers, and building its domestic defense industries. South Korea has acquired impressive new capabilities that enhance the Alliance's qualitative edge over North Korea, including F-15K fighters and AH-64E Apache heavy attack helicopters. It could further increase its edge by following through with its commitments to procure Patriot PAC-3 ballistic missile defense systems and Global Hawk, and pending procurement decisions on F-35 Joint Strike Fighters.

Combined Forces Command (CFC) continues to encourage South Korea to develop and implement new joint and combined command, control, communications, computers and intelligence, surveillance and reconnaissance (C4ISR) capabilities that are fully interoperable with the U.S. This includes a balanced approach that accounts for systems, networks, organizations, and human capital. CFC is placing special emphasis on missile defense, not only in terms of systems and capabilities, but also with regard to implementing an Alliance counter-missile strategy required for our combined defense.

5. THREE COMMANDS.

As the senior U.S. military officer in Korea, I lead three Commands: the United Nations Command (UNC), Combined Forces Command (CFC), and U.S. Forces Korea (USFK). Each Command has distinct, but mutually supporting missions and authorities.

United Nations Command. As the UNC Commander, I am charged with leading an 18-nation coalition in maintaining the Armistice to ensure a cessation of hostilities until a final peace settlement is achieved. UNC maintains the Armistice by reducing the prospect of inadvertent clashes and miscalculations particularly within the DMZ and along the Northern Limit Line. This requires that I carefully balance the UNC Armistice maintenance responsibilities with the CFC responsibilities to defend South Korea. Should conflict resume and require an international response, as the UNC Commander, I am responsible for the operational control and combat operations of UNC member nation forces. We leverage our UNC Rear Headquarters ties with Japan to promote ROK-U.S.-Japan military engagements by educating military and civilian leaders about the criticality of Japan's support to the Alliance in times of conflict. Last year saw the return of Italy to UNC, and other Sending States are increasing their participation in exercises and in our permanent UNC staff. UNC remains as vibrant today as when it was originally chartered.

U.S.-ROK Combined Forces Command. As the Commander of CFC, I am responsible for deterring North Korean aggression and, if deterrence fails, leading combined U.S.-ROK forces in the defense of the Republic of Korea. CFC enables us to organize, plan, and exercise U.S. and ROK forces to ensure that CFC is ready to "Fight Tonight" – not just a slogan, but a mindset. CFC serves a purpose beyond that of other military commands; it embodies the military dimension of the Alliance that enables Americans and Koreans to fight as a unified force.

United States Forces Korea. As the Commander of USFK, I am responsible for organizing, training, and equipping U.S. forces on the Peninsula to be agile, adaptable, and ready to support CFC and UNC, as well as U.S. Pacific Command (PACOM). USFK continues to support the ROK-U.S. Mutual Defense Treaty and serves as a stabilizing force and a visible manifestation of the U.S. commitment to South Korea. As a joint, sub-unified command of PACOM, USFK is responsible for supporting the Combatant Command's pursuit of U.S. theater and national level objectives. USFK is a member of the broader U.S. team that synchronizes and works Korea issues, including PACOM, the Joint Staff, the Office of the Secretary of Defense, the U.S. Embassy, the Interagency, and the Intelligence Community.

- **Ground Forces.** As USFK's ground component force, Eighth Army (8A) uses modernized ground combat power to deter threats to U.S. interests in Korea in full partnership with the South Korean Army. In 2013, U.S. Army Pacific established a Coordination Element on the Peninsula to provide additional synchronization. The new Army Regionally Aligned Force effort ensures CONUS-based forces are better prepared to respond to regional requirements. In late 2013 and early 2014, the Army dispatched additive rotational forces to Korea as a means to strengthen combat readiness. These rotational forces arrive in Korea fully manned and trained, and they minimize transportation costs by leaving their equipment in Korea for the next unit in the rotation. Eighth Army's enhanced readiness and presence in Korea represent a powerful U.S. commitment to deterrence and warfighting capability.

- **Air Forces.** The 7th Air Force is stationed in the Republic of Korea to apply air and space power in the Korean Theater of Operations (KTO). In 2013, 7th Air Force made advancements in command and control systems, fielding an improved version of the Theater Battle Management Core System. This new system enhances our ability to command and control thousands of coalition sorties in one of the world's most complex battle spaces. In August, the 7th Air Force Commander assumed the role of Area Air Defense Commander for the KTO. Despite resource constraints in 2013, 7th Air Force made progress in enhancing deterrence and defense through Theater Support Packages (TSP), exercises, training, and command and control enhancements. Last year, 7th Air Force hosted three TSPs augmenting our capabilities and demonstrating U.S. resolve. They continued to improve combined airpower capabilities by executing two MAX THUNDER exercises, and trained the ROK Air Force for its first-ever deployment out of country to integrate with U.S. and multinational forces.

- **Naval Forces.** The deployment and presence of the U.S. Navy's most modern combat platforms in the Pacific Region provides enhanced capabilities (air, surface, undersea) in the maritime domain. The U.S. Navy is committed to sending our most modern platforms to the Pacific Region. The routine presence in the KTO of carrier strike groups demonstrates U.S. commitment and staying power, reassures allies, and deters adversaries. The routine deployment of expeditionary strike groups allows us to conduct combined amphibious operations and advance the command and control capabilities of the ROK and U.S. Marine Air-Ground Task Force.

- **Marine Forces.** U.S. Marine Corps Forces, Korea (MARFOR-K) is a service component headquarters assigned to USFK. It coordinates support from U.S. Marine units that come primarily from the III Marine Expeditionary Force (MEF) located in Japan. MARFOR-K maintains a close relationship with the ROK Marine Corps and helps ensure that combined planning and training events are of optimal benefit to both countries. In 2013, we conducted 11 combined Korea Marine Exercise Program events that ranged from platoon to battalion size and spanned the gamut of military operations. U.S. and ROK Marine combined training includes Exercise SSANG YONG, one of the most comprehensive amphibious exercises in the world. MARFOR-K ensures that USFK remains ready to integrate forward-based U.S. Marine forces that would be critical in the early hours and days of a crisis.

- **Special Operations Forces.** Special Operations Command, Korea (SOCKOR) serves as our Theater Special Operations Command (TSOC) for Korea, providing command and control for all U.S. Special Operations Forces (SOF) in Korea. SOCKOR maintains continual engagement with the South Korean Army Special Warfare Command, its Naval Special Warfare Flotilla's SEALs, its Air Force SOF fixed wing, and its Army rotary wing SOF units. SOCKOR also serves as the UNC's subordinate headquarters that commands and controls all UN SOF during training exercises and in the event of crises or war.

6. U.S.-ROK ALLIANCE.

For over 60 years, we have stood together with the Republic of Korea in an Alliance for our common defense and increasingly rooted in mutual prosperity. We benefit from a rich combined military history and shared sacrifices. Our South Korean ally appreciates that the U.S. provided the security and assistance that enabled South Korea's hard earned success and liberty. Today, the Alliance stands as one of history's strongest and most effective military partnerships, one that has evolved to include regional and global security interests. In the coming year, we will continue to collaborate in addressing the challenges of Alliance transformation, enhancing counter-provocation capability, and implementing the counter missile strategy consistent with the Revised Missile Guidelines (RMG) and the bilateral Tailored Deterrence Strategy (TDS).

Strong Relationships. Our greatest strength rests in our close, daily cooperation built on trust. We have transparent and candid relationships that enable our ability to address tough warfighting and interoperability issues. We will continue to nurture the strong relationships that provide us with the mutual understanding, respect, and habits of cooperation required to preserve decision space and options during provocations or crisis.

Alliance Transformation. The U.S. Office of the Secretary of Defense and ROK Ministry of National Defense are holding working group meetings to clarify South Korea's proposed conditions and prerequisites for wartime operational control (OPCON) transition and to review the bilaterally agreed upon pathway to OPCON transition in Strategic Alliance 2015. As the bilateral group continues its work, I remain focused on our combined readiness, and especially on enhancing the critical South Korean military capabilities identified in Strategic Alliance 2015. As they deliberate, we remain committed to preserving the benefits and advantages of being combined while ensuring that we are positioning the Alliance for long-term sustainability and operational effectiveness, and that we are doing so in a fiscally-sound manner.

Authorities and Consultation. Our consultative procedures remain robust and through these mechanisms, including the annual Security Consultative Meeting (SCM) and Military Committee Meeting (MCM), we continue to deepen our relationships and ensure that our military receives synchronized national-level direction. Our bilateral strategic documents define U.S. authorities within the Alliance and codify authorities for the Command to plan, train, and maintain readiness, as well as assume command should South Korea request that we do so in times of crises or war. These ensure the U.S. retains a voice and a stake in decisions and actions taken on the Korean Peninsula.

Burden Sharing. Earlier this year, the Alliance concluded a new cost sharing agreement called the Special Measures Agreement (SMA), which will be in effect through 2018. Under the SMA, South Korea will help offset the costs of stationing U.S. forces in Korea by providing support for labor, supplies, services, and construction. For 2014, Seoul will provide $867 million in cost sharing support. SMA contributions also stimulate the South Korean economy through salaries and benefits to host nation workers, supply and service contracts, and local construction work. SMA support plays a critical role in developing and maintaining force readiness.

Counter Missile Capabilities. The United States and South Korea are implementing a comprehensive Alliance counter missile strategy based on detecting, defending, disrupting, and destroying North Korean missile threats. The strategy calls for the development of new South Korean ballistic missiles with increased ranges as well as enhanced ISR capabilities, including unmanned aerial vehicles. South Korea continues to implement the Revised Missile Guidelines (RMG), an important element in increasing Alliance capabilities to defend both South Korea and the United States. While we are making progress in implementing the RMG and countering the North Korean missile threat, we must continue to work toward enacting combined command and control processes to integrate our respective capabilities.

Tailored Deterrence. In October 2013, the U.S. Secretary of Defense and ROK Minister of National Defense signed the bilateral Tailored Deterrence Strategy (TDS). The TDS is a significant milestone in the U.S.-ROK security relationship, and establishes an Alliance framework for ensuring deterrence against North Korean nuclear and weapons of mass destruction (WMD) threat scenarios. The TDS is not an operational plan, nor does it call for preemptive strikes or specific responses to North Korean actions. The TDS identifies a variety of capabilities that allow the Alliance to explore and implement options to enhance deterrence.

Operationalizing Deterrence. In 2013, U.S. Pacific Command and U.S. Strategic Command dispatched strategic platforms to the KTO, including Carrier Strike Groups, Ohio Class guided-missile and Los Angeles Class attack submarines, F-22 fighters, and B-52 and B-2 bombers. These operations reassured the South Korean people of our commitment and provided a tangible demonstration of extended deterrence.

Exercises. Exercising our joint, combined, and multinational forces is an important component of readiness and is fundamental to sustaining and strengthening the Alliance. CFC and the ROK Joint

Chiefs of Staff conduct three major annual exercises. Exercises KEY RESOLVE and FOAL EAGLE (Feb/Mar) and ULCHI FREEDOM GUARDIAN (Aug) provide the primary and most effective means to ensure combined readiness and deterrence – we must sustain them despite budget and resource constraints. Our exercises are a key opportunity to work through warfighting and interoperability issues, and enable the Alliance to adapt to the changing strategic environment, including progressing toward South Korean leadership in the defense of the Peninsula.

Readiness and Challenges. As a global military priority – second only to Afghanistan – and despite fiscal and resource limitations, we have maintained a high state of readiness. However, I am concerned about shortfalls in critical areas including C4ISR, missile defense, critical munitions, and the readiness of follow-on forces. North Korea's forward deployed posture and demonstrated expertise in denial and deception present significant challenges. We can meet these challenges better by increasing ISR assets and analytic capability, and we are working to do so both with our on-Peninsula U.S. forces and ROK forces. I am encouraged by South Korean efforts to address missile defense limitations; however, effective solutions require a composite of integrated systems and capabilities. Next, we do not have sufficient stocks of some critical munitions and thus need to increase and maintain our on-Peninsula stock. Finally, fiscal limitations will impact the training and readiness of follow-on forces. Any delay in the arrival or reduction in readiness of these forces would lengthen the time required to accomplish key missions in crisis or war, likely resulting in higher civilian and military casualties.

A Bright Future Together. President Obama and President Park reaffirmed last year the "2009 Joint Vision for the Alliance of the United States of America and the Republic of Korea." This landmark vision lays out an ambitious Alliance expansion. We will continue to encourage South Korea to develop stronger military-to-military relations with our other key allies and partners in the region. The Republic of Korea, as the 12th largest economy in the world with a modern military, is seeking to expand its role

15

in regional and international security, and we look forward to increasing our global partnership as outlined in the 2009 Joint Vision statement.

7. VISION 2014 AND PRIORITIES.

The Command will work to implement my priorities of strengthening the Alliance, maintaining the Armistice, and taking care of our people. We will remain vigilant against the North Korean threat, and we will strive to create enduring regional and global stability and prosperity.

My priorities are straightforward: Sustain and Strengthen the Alliance; Maintain the Armistice: Deter and Defeat Aggression – Be Ready to "Fight Tonight"; Transform the Alliance; Sustain Force and Family Readiness; and Enhance the UNC, CFC, and USFK Team.

Sustain and Strengthen the Alliance. America is fortunate to have committed and capable friends, and I have had the privilege of working alongside many of our Allies across a range of circumstances. This is my first time serving in South Korea. The South Korean military is impressive and is one of the most capable and best trained militaries in the world. South Korea is a true ally, willing to share burdens and make sacrifices in pursuit of our common values and interests. The coming year will provide an opportunity to strengthen our Alliance. Together, our Alliance can ensure a strong and effective deterrence posture so that Pyongyang never misjudges our role, our commitment, or our capability to respond to aggression. We are also working to expand the scope of trilateral security cooperation between the United States, South Korea, and Japan, thereby sending a strong message to Pyongyang. Relationships matter, and it is our people who more than anything else make possible our unity of purpose and action. So, we will reinforce the principle of working toward Alliance solutions to Alliance issues, and in the spirit of the Alliance, we will move "Forward Together."

Maintain the Armistice: Deter and Defeat Aggression – Be Ready to "Fight Tonight." Tightly linked to strengthening the Alliance is the imperative of maintaining the Armistice and deterring

16

aggression. Being ready to "Fight Tonight" means that if deterrence fails, the Alliance is ready to defeat aggression. The key to readiness is ensuring that U.S. and ROK forces are properly trained and equipped, and that follow-on forces are fully trained and capable of deploying on a tight timeline. Failure to maintain a high level of readiness leads to strategic risk against a well-armed North Korea possessing asymmetric capabilities. Despite fiscal and resource limitations, the forces in Korea maintain a high state of readiness.

Alliance Transformation. We will continue to press forward on Alliance transformation, focusing on achieving the goals set forth in Strategic Alliance 2015 (SA 2015), the roadmap for Alliance transformation into a ROK-led command structure. We designed SA 2015 to set conditions for a successful, enduring, and stronger Alliance. We must modernize our force posture and command and control to adapt to the changing NK threat in a manner that is sustainable and operationally effective. We will place increased emphasis on enhancing our cyber and special operations capabilities and will study lessons learned and technological advancements for application in the Korean Theater.

Sustain Force and Family Readiness. My final two priorities are linked -- sustaining force and family readiness is enabled by our efforts to enhance the team. The challenge of limited warning and decision space increases the criticality of training and readiness. Readiness applies not only to our combat forces but our families as well. Our people are most effective when their families are cared for and in balance. The personnel turbulence caused by one-year tours and our nation's fiscal issues compound the magnitude of this challenge. We are working to address the issue of personnel turbulence by being very discerning with how we allocate command-sponsored tours and in the use of rotational forces. I ask for your assistance in supporting the best force we can sustain in Korea and the corresponding support for our families.

Enhance the UNC, CFC, and USFK Team. I am instilling a command climate based on valued team members, teamwork, standards, discipline, and balanced lives. This includes encouraging spiritual, family, physical, professional, and personal balance and resilience. My vision for our command climate is upholding the covenant between the leader and the led. And one of the most important aspects of leading and taking care of our Service Members is my commitment to combating sexual assault and sexual harassment. We are unwavering in our commitment to doing so, and I know this resonates at every level of our Command. In and of itself, sexual assault is deplorable and unacceptable, and undermines the trust that is required to operate effectively as a team.

8. CLOSING.

The U.S.-ROK Alliance remains strong with an important future. The UNC/CFC/USFK Command and its dedicated men and women are ready every day to deter the North Korean threat, and if necessary, they are ready to fight and win. I am honored to have the opportunity to lead this dedicated joint, combined, and multinational force in one of the most vital regions of the world. We have a serious mission against a real threat, and as the USFK Commander, I deeply appreciate each American who has volunteered to serve far from home to support a close ally, protect American interests, and demonstrate American leadership and willingness to stand up to those who would threaten our way of life. Mr. Chairman, again, thank you for this chance to meet with you and your Committee, and I look forward to working together.